D0762290

CALGARY PUBLIC LIBRARY

FEB   2017

Sunflower

LIFE CYCLES

Words in **bold** can be found in the glossary on page 24.

©2016
Book Life
King's Lynn
Norfolk PE30 4LS

ISBN: 978-1-910512-49-4

Written by:
Grace Jones
Edited by:
Harriet Brundle
Designed by:
Matt Rumbelow

A catalogue record for this book
is available from the British Library.

All rights reserved
Printed in China

Sunflower

What is a Life Cycle?

All animals, plants and humans go through different stages of their life as they grow and change. This is called a **life cycle**.

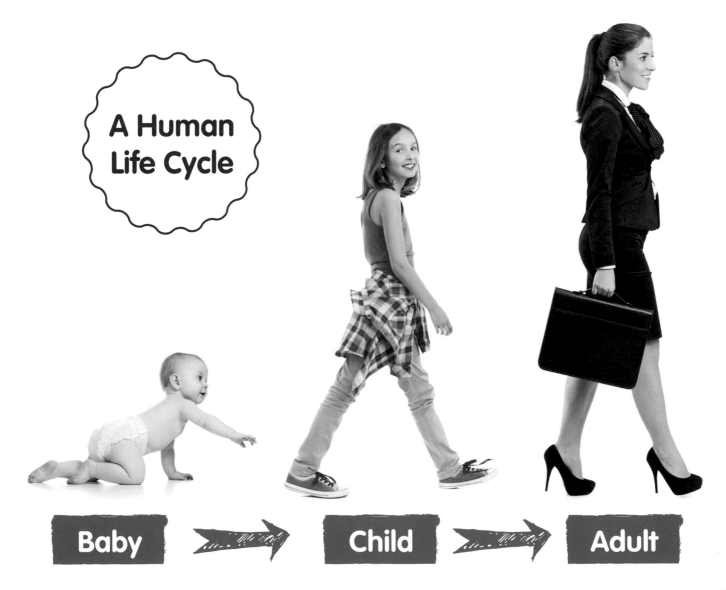

A Human Life Cycle

Baby ➤ Child ➤ Adult

What is a Sunflower?

A sunflower is a tall plant that is mainly found in North America, but it can be found all over the world, too. Sunflowers usually have flowers with bright yellow petals on them.

Petals

Sunflower Plant

Seeds

Sunflower seeds are blown by the wind or carried by insects onto soil on the ground.

The seed stays buried in the **soil** all winter long.

Sunflower Seeds

Sunflower
Seed

Sunflower seeds need warmth from the sun and water from the rain to help them grow. In springtime, when the weather is warmer, the sunflower seeds start to change.

Roots and Shoots

With enough sunshine and water, the seed splits open and a tiny root grows downwards into the soil. The root is the part of the plant that takes in important **minerals** and water from the soil.

Seed

Root

A small shoot also sprouts from the seed and grows upwards. When roots and shoots start to grow from a seed, the seed has **germinated**.

❀
Roots grow downwards into the soil and shoots grow upwards into the air.
❀

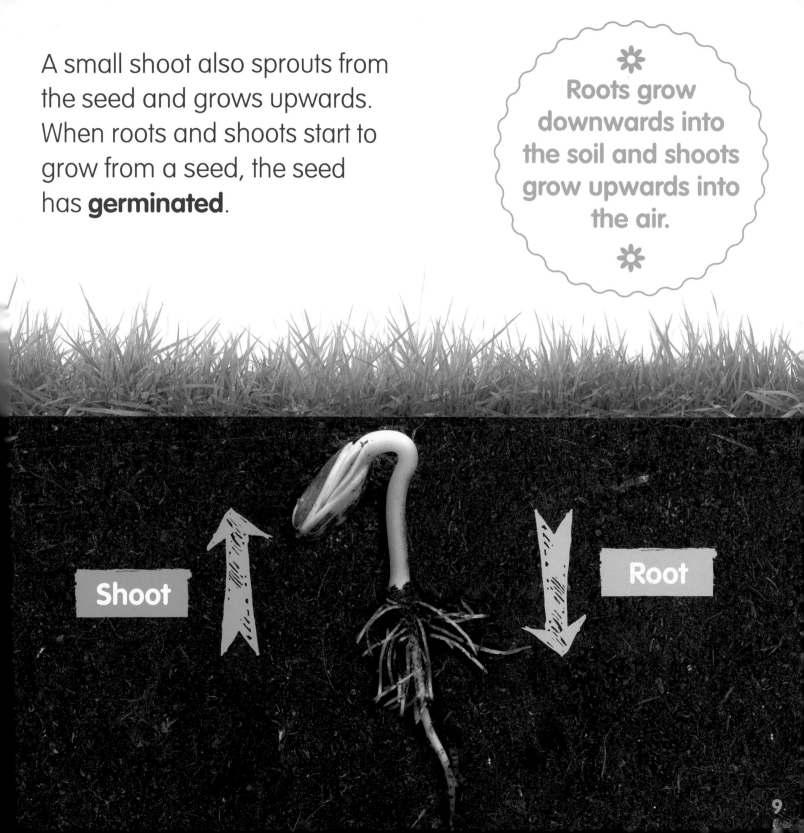

Shoot

Root

9

Growing Roots and Shoots

After around two weeks, the tiny **seedling** pushes up and out of the soil to try and find the sunlight above the ground.

Seedling

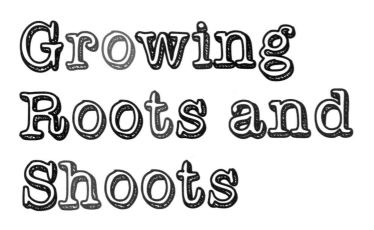

More roots begin to grow from the first root down into the soil.

The roots are very strong and stop the seedling from blowing away in the wind.

Roots work just like an anchor on a boat, which helps to keep it from floating away!

Stem

The long, thin part of the sunflower that grows above the ground is called its stem. Sunflower stems are strong to keep the plant standing upright as it grows taller.

Stem

Stems carry water
and minerals up
from the roots to
the rest of the plant,
much like a straw!

Leaves and Buds

As the seedling gets bigger, leaves start to grow from the stem of the plant. Leaves collect important **vitamins** from the sunlight to give the plant energy to help it grow.

Leaves

Stem

A **bud** starts to grow at the top of the stem. The bud is the part of the sunflower plant where a flower will grow.

Bud

Sunflowers

The sunflower bud starts to open out into a flower. After around eight weeks of growing, the tiny seed has grown into a beautiful sunflower!

Opening Bud

Each flower head has lots of tiny flowers inside it. They also have more sunflower seeds in the middle of them. The seeds are blown away by the wind and its life cycle begins once more.

Flowers

Seeds

Sunflower Superfoods!

A sunflower's seeds can be eaten by humans as a healthy snack because they contain lots of vitamins.

Sunflower seeds are sometimes baked in bread.

Sunflower oil is used to cook with. It is a healthier option to most other oils as it contains less fat.

World Record Breakers

World's Tallest Sunflower

Grown in: Kaarst, Germany.
Height: 9.17 metres.

Fun Fact: The world's tallest sunflower is almost twice as big as the world's tallest giraffe!

9.17m

World's Most Famous Sunflower Painting:
Van Gogh's 'Vase with Fifteen Sunflowers'.

Fun Fact: The painting last sold in 1987 for a whopping 24 million pounds!

Life Cycle of a Sunflower

1 A seed is buried in the soil.

2 Roots and shoots sprout out of the seed.

LIFE CYCLES

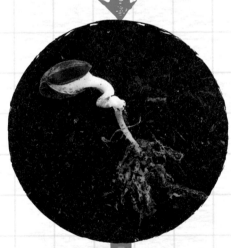

4 The buds open up and the plant flowers.

3 Leaves and buds grow from the stem.

Grow Your Own!

1. Buy some sunflower seeds from your nearest supermarket or garden centre.

2. In springtime, plant the seeds 1 cm under the soil inside a plant pot.

3. Leave the pot in a sunny area in your garden and water gently with a watering can when the soil gets dry.

4. Watch your sunflower plant grow!

Glossary

Bud: a small shoot that grows into a flower.

Germinated: when roots and shoots start to grow from the seed.

Minerals: important things a plant, animal or human needs to grow.

Seedling: a young plant.

Soil: tiny pieces of broken stone, dead plants and sand.

Vitamins: important things a plant, animal or human needs to grow.

Index

Photo Credits

Photocredits: Abbreviations: l-left, r-right, b-bottom, t-top, c-centre, m-middle. All images are courtesy of Shutterstock.com.
Front Cover — Ian 2010. 1 – Ian 2010. 2 - cooperr. 3 - Thomas M Perkins. 4l - Oksana Kuzmina. 4m - studioloco. 4r - Ljupco Smokovski. 5 - Ian 2010. 6l - Jiri Hera. 6m - Ian 2010. 6r - Jaimie Duplass. 7l - gornjak. 7r - Idphotoro. 8c - surassawadee. 8 - Aksenenko Olga. 8t - antpkr. 9 - Aksenenko Olga. 9t - antpkr. 9c - Bogdan Wankowicz. 10 - Aksenenko Olga. 10t - antpkr. 10r - Filipe B. Varela. 11 - Filipe B. Varela. 11inset - Yarkovoy. 12 - Valentina Razumova. 13 - Serhiy Kobyakov. 15 - Krisdayod. 16 - toey19863. 17 - pkproject. 18 - Nils Z. 18t - DenisNata. 19 - Oksana Shufrych. 20 - Alexander Kazantsev. 21 - gillmar. 22t - Jiri Hera. 22r - surassawadee. 22b - Krisdayod. 22l - pkproject. 24 - Valentina Razumova.